A LETTERation Beginning Sounds and Rhymes Phonemic Awareness Activity

Created by Catherine Thompson-Alexander

All Rights Reserves
Copyright 2002 Effective Publications

Reproduction in any manner, in whole or in part, in English or in other languages, or otherwise without written permission of the publisher is prohibited.

For Information, write:
Effective Publications
3506 Highway 6 South, # 335
Sugar Land, TX 77478
281-261-7201

ISBN: 0-9726522-0-5
Printed in the United States of America

Notes:

Directions:

First: Introduce the sound card of the letter targeted. Say the name of the letter. The students should repeat the name of the letter.

Second: Introduce the words that are illustrated for the letter. Explain that these words begin with the letter's sound. The students should repeat the words listed that begin with the target letter.

Third: Ask the students to think of other words that begin with that sound. The teacher may need to prompt the students by naming categories that the words belong. A "prompt" card is provided to aid the teacher. The teacher may want the children to listen and repeat the words that begin with the target sound for auditory bombardment.

Fourth: For the vowel sounds, the teacher will be generating rhyming words. Explain that you are going to say some words that can be rhymed. Ask the students to form as many words as possible that rhyme with the word. To reduce the level of difficulty, ask the children to repeat the rhyming words.

Aa   Long Vowel Sound   1a

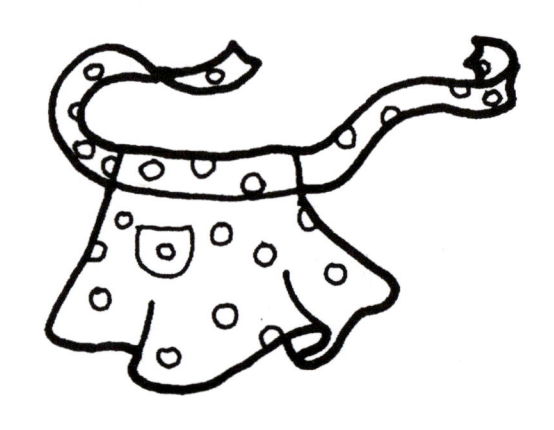

Apron    **Acorn**    **Anchor**

Aa Long Vowel Sound Word 1b

1) Ask students to form words that begin with the long vowel sound of A.
Examples:

Aim	Aiming	Ate	April	Ace	Able
Aid	Age	Ache	Apricot	Acorn	Acre
Ape	Apron	Agent	Agency	Anchor	Anger

2) Ask students to form words that rhyme with the words listed below:
Ace – base, brace, case, chase, face, grace, lace, pace, place, race, space, trace, vase
Ache – bake, cake, brake, fake, lake, make, rake, sake, shake, snake, steak, take
Ate - bait, date, fate, gate, late, plate, rate, skate, state, straight, wait, eight, Kate
Age – cage, gauge, page, rage, sage, wage, stage, teenage, backstage, bird cage
Aid – fade, laid, made, wade, shade, braid, grade, blade, played, jade, paid, trade
Ail – pail, sail, tale, tail, rail, nail, mail, Gale, snail, trail, frail, Dale, whale, scale

Aa Short Vowel Sound   2a

Apple   **Ant**   **Alligator**

Aa Short Vowel Sound Word List 2b

1) Ask students to form words that begin with the short vowel sound of A.
Examples:

Am	Afternoon	Antler	Accent	An	Absent
Act	Amber	Ask	Anthill	Adam	At
Acting	Active	Answer	Ax	Apple juice	Antelope

2) Ask students to form words that rhyme with the words listed below:

Am – Sam, ram, Pam, jam, slam, yam, clam, cram, ham, swam, wham, tram, scam
At – bat, cat, rat, sat, pat, mat, chat, that, flat, slat, hat, splat, hardhat, wildcat
An - pan, ran, can, Dan, fan, man, tan, van, than, Anne, ban, Jan, plan, Stan
Add – sad, mad, pad, dad, glad, had, lad, bad, plaid, Chad, grad, clad
Back – Jack, lack, rack, sack, tack, crack, track, shack, black, slack, stack
Bag – gag, rag, drag, nag, tag, brag, flag, sag, lag, shag, snag, wag, zag
Map – cap, rap, tap, sap, nap, lap, clap, flap, snap, wrap, trap, gap, scrap, strap

Bb   B Sound   3a

Bird   **B**utterfly   **B**ananas

Bb B Sound Word List

1) Ask students to form words that begin with the B sound.
Examples:

Banana	Bake	Boss	Baggage	Bus	Band
Bug	Baseball	Bike	Bank	Bud	Basement
Bird	Barn	Buck	Basket	Bull	Base
Bump	Bedroom	Bunny	Bass	Bunch	Bedtime
Bed	Bat	Burst	Billfold	Beard	Bath
Buy	Birthday	Button	Beach	Buzz	Birdhouse
Busy	Bean	Boo	Biscuit	Butter	Bell
Buffalo	Border	Boy	Belt	Bulldozer	Bucket
Boat	Big	Bow	Building	Bath	Best
Builder	Bulldog	Bottle	Bite	Beaver	Buzzing
Berry	Boil	Bacon	Beautiful	Back	Bone
Baby	Barber	Book	Boot	Borrow	Both

Cc   C Sound   4a

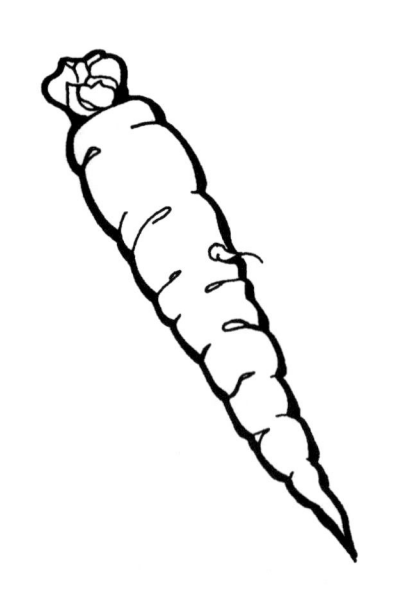

Cake   **C**arrot   **C**amel

Cc   C Sound Word List   4b

1) Ask students to form words that begin with the C sound.
Examples:

Can	Coat	Captain	Carnival	Comb	Cob
Castle	Come	Corn	Coin	Cartoon	Comic
Candy	Cold	Cattle	Collect	Cow	Cone
Coffee	Computer	Coach	Cook	Collar	Contest
Cab	Couch	Color	Cost	Cage	Cough
Copy	Cookie	Cap	Cool	Corner	Cub
Cape	Cup	Costume	Could	Cane	Cut
Cousin	Consonant	Care	Curl	Calendar	Compare
Cart	Cabin	Camera	Container	Case	Cabbage
Cowboy	Comfortable	Cash	Caboose	Cotton	Careful
Cave	Camel	Card	Cannot	Cause	Candle
Count	Can't	Counter	Cover	Cozy	Correct

Dd D Sound   5a

Dog   **Dinosaur**   **Duckling**

Dd D Sound Word List 5b

1) Ask students to form words that begin with the D sound.
Examples:

Dad	Dust	Dirt	Dent	Date	Dove
Dump	Dollar	Damp	Down	Dinosaur	Duck
Dan	Daisy	Dishtowel	Daycare	Dark	Daughter
Dishwasher	Delicious	Date	Dentist	Dump truck	Dice
Day	Dessert	Dusty	Different	Deer	Dial
Difficult	Diana	Deck	Diet	Dumbo	Debbie
Den	Dinner	Decorate	Dock	Desk	Distance
Deep	Doll	Dice	Dizzy	Dozer	Due
Dig	Doctor	Diver	Drum	Dime	Dolphin
Dessert	Drive	Dip	Donkey	Desert	Drink
Dish	Double	Daily	Denver	Dive	Doughnut
Dallas	Dream	Do	Dozen	Damage	Draw
Dot	Dusting	Dancer	Dress		

Ee Long Vowel Sound 6a

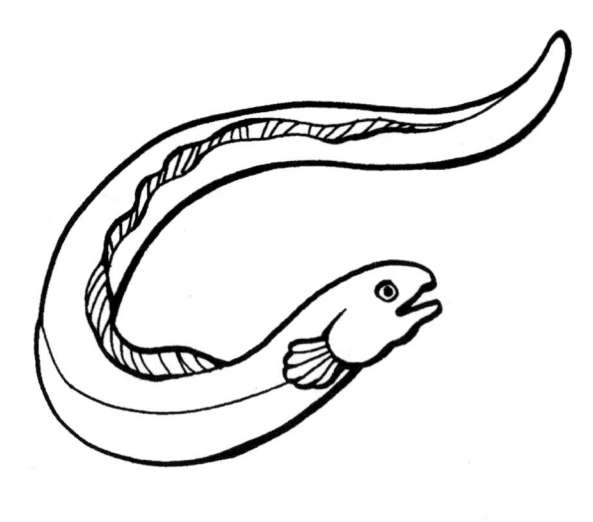

Eagle **Eel** **Eat**

Ee Long Vowel Sound Word List 6b

1) Ask students to form words that begin with the long vowel sound of E.
Examples:

East	Easy	Easily	Eat	Eve	Even
Evening	Each	Equal	Either	Eastern	Event

2) Ask students to form words that rhyme with the words listed below:

Ease – breeze, cheese, fees, fleas, freeze, keys, knees, please, seas, sees, sneeze, skis

Eat – beat, cheat, feet, fleet, greet, heat, meat, meet, neat, seat, sheet, sleet, street, suite, sweet, treat, wheat, Pete, tweet

Bean – clean, green, lean, mean, queen, scene, screen, seen, jean, teen, dean

Beep - deep, heap, jeep, keep, leap, peep, sleep, sheep, steep, cheap, sweep, weep

Be – bee, key, sea, see, flea, fee, he, me, tree, we, free, she, tea, knee, she, three

Each – beach, reach, teach, bleach, leach, peach, screech, speech

Ee Short Vowel Sound 7a

Egg   **E**lephant   **E**lbow

Ee Short Vowel Sound Word List   7b

1) Ask students to form words that begin with the short vowel sound of E.
Examples:

Enter	Elbow	Everybody	Energy	Exit	Election
Excellent	Engine	Echo	Elevator	Enjoy	Envelope
Edge	Else	Enemy	Every	Empty	End

2) Ask students to form words that rhyme with the words listed below:

Ed – bed, fed, head, led, lead, red, said, shed, dead, sped, spread, thread, bread
Bell – cell, fell, jell, sell, shell, smell, swell, tell, yell, dwell, spell, well, gel
Egg – leg, Meg, peg, Greg, beg
Bet – debt, jet, met, set, net, wet, sweat, pet, let, vet, yet, get, threat

Ff F Sound 8a

Fish   **Fireman**   **Fork**

Ff F Sound Word List 8b

1) Ask students to form words that begin with the F sound.
Examples:

Face	Food	Fudge	Fasten	Fan	Four
Famous	Favor	Farm	Five	Fancy	Firefly
Fish	Fork	Farmer	Fire Truck	Feed	Fever
Farming	Fishing	Feet	Football	Farmhouse	Forget
Fern	Feather	Father	Forgot	Fence	Fell
Final	Fossil	Film	Fireman	Forest	Fourteen
Fox	Fall	Funny	Faucet	Fur	Far
Fold	First Aid	Fire	Fast	Fizz	Foot
Finger	Few	Full	Fizzle	Fairy	Fight
Fabric	Focus	Fit	Fix	Finish	Field
Feel	Falling	Firm	First	Follow	Forty
Fashion	File	Filling	Fin	Fiddle	Fountain

Gg   G Sound

9a

Goose   **G**as   **G**oat

Gg G Sound Word List

1) Ask students to form words that begin with the G sound.
Examples:

Gate	Good	Garage	Golden	Game	Got
Garlic	Good-bye	Gap	Gown	Gary	Gopher
Gas	Guess	Gazelle	Guide	Gave	Guest
Getting	Gift	Geese	Get	Gifted	Guppy
Ghost	Guilt	Given	Gorilla	Goal	Gulp
Giving	Government	Go	Gum	Goal Post	Governor
Give	Guy	Goalie	Garden Hose	Gold	Gallon
Gobble	Gasoline	Golf	Gallop	Go-Cart	Gather
Gone	Garden	Going	Gardening	Grab	Green
Gown	Glass	Garbage	Gayle	Greg	Grass
Glove	Glow	Glue	Grab	Grape	Grasshopper

Hh   H Sound

10a

_H_orse **_H_ammer** **_H_ouse**

Hh   H Sound Word List   10b

1) Ask students to form words that begin with the H sound.
Examples:

Had	Head	Hi	Hit	Hair	Heap
Hers	Hive	Half	Hear	Hid	Ho
Ham	Heart	Hide	Hope	Hang	Heat
High	Hog	Heel	Hike	Hold	Horse
Has	Height	Hill	Hole	Hatch	Help
Him	Home	Hearing	Heather	House	Hello
Haul	Hen	Hint	Honk	Have	Her
Hip	Hood	Hawk	Herd	His	Hoof
Hay	Here	Hiss	Hook	Hamster	Hoop
Hiding	Hug	Hammer	Horn	Headache	Henry
Hanger	Hose	Hope	Hard	Handle	Hidden
Healthy	Hiding	Henry	Harry	Howdy	Hurry

Ii Long Vowel Sound 11a

Ice Skates   **Ice Cream**   **Ivy**

Ii   Long Vowel Sound Word List   11b

1) Ask students to form words that begin with the long vowel sound of I.
Examples:

Ice Cream	Icicle	I	I'm	Ice Age
I-MAX	Iceland	Icing	ID	Ivory

2) Ask students to form words that rhyme with the words listed below:
Ice – dice, lice, mice, nice, price, rice, slice, spice, twice, vice, splice
Bite – bright, fight, height, kite, knight, light, might, night, quite, right, sight, white
Hide - glide, guide, pride, ride, side, slide, stride, tide, wide, bride, dried, glide
Dime – chime, time, rhyme, crime, slime, lime, I'm, prime, grime, climb
I – try, my, lie, die, cry, fly, guy, pie, rye, sigh, tie, dry, fry, thigh, shy, hi, high
Bike – Mike, hike, like, pike, spike

Ii Short Vowel Sound 12a

Igloo **Indian** **Insect**

Ii Short Vowel Sound Word List   12b

1) Ask students to form words that begin with the short vowel sound of I.
Examples:

| Is | Ill | Infant | Inside | Inch | Index |
| Inhale | Instrument | It | Inn | Insect | Into |

2) Ask students to form words that rhyme with the words listed below:
It – bit, fit, hit, kit, knit, lit, mitt, pit, quit, sit, skit, slit, split, spit, wit, grit
Ill – chill, bill, dill, drill, fill, gill, grill, hill, Jill, mill, pill, skill , spill, still, thrill
In – bin, chin, din, fin, grin, kin, pin, skin, spin, thin, tin, twin, win, Lynn
Kick – sick, chick, lick, Rick, tick, brick, thick, click, slick, nick, pick quick, stick
Dip – lip, rip, sip, tip, nip, whip, ship, chip, clip, slip, flip, drip, trip, grip, zip
Dim – Kim, rim, Tim, trim, slim, swim, him, Jim, brim, limb, prim, skim, whim

Jj J Sound 13a

Jump   **Jet**   **Jar**

Jj   J Sound Word List

1) Ask students to form words that begin with the J sound.
Examples:

Jack	Joke	Japan	Juicy	Jam	Joy
Jelly	Jumbo	Jane	Judge	Jenny	Jumper
Jar	Jug	Jerry	June Bug	Jaw	Juice
Jewel	Jungle	Jazz	Jump	Jiggle	Junior
Jeans	Jumped	Jigsaw	Justin	Jeep	June
Jimmy	Jellybeans	Jell	Just	Jolly	Jellyfish
Jill	Jacket	Journey	Jennifer	Jim	Jaguar
Journal	Jackpot	Job	Janet	Joyful	Jiffy
Joe	Jamie	Juggle	Judy	Jennifer	Jacket

Kk K Sound 14a

Kick   **K**angaroo   **K**itten

Kk K Sound Word List   14b

1) Ask students to form words that begin with the K sound.
Examples:

Key	Kit	Keyboard	Kitten	Kick	Kite
Key chain	Kangaroo	Kicked	Keep	Kickball	Kentucky
Kid	Kelly	Kicker	Kindergarten	Ken	Keeping
Kidding	Kayak	Kept	Kenny	Kindness	Kiss
Kay	Kermit	Kingdom	Kind	Keep	Ketchup
Kitchen	Kim	Karate	Kiwi	Kyle	Kirk
Kevin	Kansas	King	Key-hole	Key-board	Kernel

Ll   L Sound   15a

Lamp   **Lion**   **Leaf**

Ll   L Sound Word List   15b

1) Ask students to form words that begin with the L sound.
Examples:

Lace	Left	Luck	Locker	Lemon	Leg
Lip	Lotion	Lag	Length	Lunch	Lightning
Less	Lit	Lung	Lettuce	Lake	Lay
Load	Laundry	Lamb	Lid	Ladder	Ladybug
Lamp	Leak	Log	Lemonade	Land	Life
Long	Letter	Lane	Lift	Loose	Lion
Lap	Light	Lizard	Listen	Large	Leash
Loud	Lobster	Last	Leave	Lime	Lifeguard
Late	Line	Low	Lipstick	Later	Lock
Lady	Leader	Lazy	Leap	Laugh	Love

Mm   M Sound

16a

Mouse　　　**Mittens**　　　**Monkey**

Mm M Sound Word List   16b

1) Ask students to form words that begin with the M sound.
Examples:

Mad	Mile	Much	Marriage	Mail	Milk
Mud	Mud	Main	Mind	Mug	Mug
Make	Mine	Mush	Middle	Mall	Mint
Must	My	Malt	Miss	Mutt	Machine
Man	Missed	My	Magnet	Map	Men
Machine	Move	March	Mitt	Magnet	Mouse
Mash	Mix	Manners	Mop	Match	Mixed
Many	Mouth	Math	Mold	Marbles	Moose
Matt	Mole	Market	Muffin	Mike	Meat
Mom	Melt	Movie	Monkey	Milk	Month
Mountain	Mirror	Mile	May	Mother	Minute
Mind	Meal	Money	Mermaid	Mice	Moon

Nn   N Sound   17a

Nest   **Numbers**   **Net**

Nn N Sound Word List 17b

1) Ask students to form words that begin with the N sound.
Examples:.

Nail	None	Navy	Nickel	Name	Noon
Nearly	Nickname	Nap	North	Necklace	Nightgown
Near	Nose	Necktie	Nineteen	Neat	Not
Needle	Ninety	Neck	Note	Neighbor	Noodle
Need	Noun	Neither	Normal	Neil	Nurse
Neon	North Pole	Nerve	Nut	Nephew	Nothing
Nest	Nancy	Never	Number	Net	Napkin
New York	Natural	New	Narrow	New Year	Nevada
Nice	Night	Nine	Next	Nicholas	Nod

Oo Long Vowel Sound 18a

Over   **O**ld   **O**veralls

Oo Long Vowel Sound Word — 18b

1) Ask students to form words that begin with the long vowel sound of O.
Examples:

Oh	Odor	Oat	Oak	Only	Open
Oatmeal	Oval	Obey	Opener	Own	Overalls

2) Ask students to form words that rhyme with the words listed below:

Old – bold, cold, fold, gold, hold, mold, rolled, sold, strolled, told, scold, polled
Owes – bows, blows, chose, close, crows, doze, flows, froze, glows, goes, grows, hose, knows, mows, nose, owes, toes, rose, sews, shows, throws, snows, sews, those
Oak – broke , choke, croak, joke, poke, smoke, soak, spoke, stroke, woke, Coke
Oat – boat, float, gloat, goat, note, quote, wrote, throat, tote, vote, coat, dote, moat
Owed – road, mowed, showed, load, sewed, toad, flowed, glowed, code, slowed
Oh – so, go, show, Joe, low, mow, row, toe, grow, flow, slow, blow, bow, crow, no
Own – loan, flown, groan, moan, clone, bone, cone, phone, Joan, known, shown

Oo   Short Vowel Sound   19a

Octopus   **October**   **Ostrich**

Oo Short Vowel Sound Word List   19b

1) Ask students to form words that begin with the short vowel sound of O.
Examples:

On	Odd	Onset	Office	Object	Olive
Observe	Officer	Ox	Onward	Occupy	Operate
Otter	Obstacle	October	Operation	Octopus	Off

2) Ask students to form words that rhyme with the words listed below:

Fog – bog, dog, frog, hog, jog, log, clog, bulldog, bullfrog, leapfrog

Ought – bought, brought, clot, cot, dot, got, hot, knot, lot, plot, pot, rot, shot, slot, spot, squat, tot, trot, watt, yacht, blot, caught, fought, jot, Scott, taught, thought

Sock – dock, rock, tock, block, shock, clock, flock, smock, chalk, hawk, knock

On – fawn, gone, dawn, lawn, Ron, Shawn, drawn, John, pawn, swan, yawn

Odd – cod, nod, rod, sod, Tod, trod, plod, quad, sawed, squad, wad

Hop – pop, plop, shop, flop, stop, mop, top, chop, cop, crop, drop, swap

Pp P Sound

20a

Pear   Penguin   Paint

Pp   P Sound Word List   20b

1) Ask students to form words that begin with the P sound.
Examples:

Pack	Perch	Panda	Pepper	Pad	Pet
Papa	Pancake	Page	Peach	Paper	Peacock
Paid	Pick	Parade	Perfume	Pail	Pie
Parent	Pickle	Pain	Pig	Parrot	Picnic
Paint	Pill	Partner	Pilot	Pair	Pin
Pattern	Pitcher	Palm	Pinch	Package	Pocket
Pam	Pine	Peanuts	Police	Pan	Pink
Pecan	Pony	Pant	Point	Pedal	Popcorn
Park	Poke	Pencil	Poster	Pass	Pole
Penny	Pumpkin	Past	Pond	People	Puppy

Qq   Q Sound   21a

Quack   **Queen**   **Quarterback**

Qq Q Sound Word List   21b

1) Ask students to form words that begin with the Q sound.
Examples:

Quart	Quick	Quarrel	Quality	Quartet	Quicksand
Quantity	Question	Quilt	Quite	Question	Quarterback

Rr R Sound   22a

Ring   **Rain**   **Rabbit**

Rr R Sound Word List 22b

1) Ask students to form words that begin with the R sound.
Examples:

Race	Ring	Radish	Rotten	Rack	Rip
Rainbow	Rowboat	Raft	Ripe	Raincoat	Ruby
Rag	Rise	Raisin	Ruling	Rail	Risk
Randy	Rub	Rain	Road	Radio	Really
Raise	Roast	Rattle	Rebecca	Rake	Robe
Reason	Rodeo	Ram	Rod	Relax	Rocket
Ramp	Roll	Relief	Ruffle	Ran	Roof
Reptile	Ruling	Ranch	Room	Rescue	Roofing
Rang	Rope	Ribbon	Roping	Rash	Roots
Robot	Racing	Rat	Rest	Ruler	Run
Reach	Ride	Rug	Rose	Red	Rick
Round	Right	Read	Raccoon	Racket	Rhyme

Ss   S Sound   23a

Seal   **Sun**   **Socks**

Ss S Sound Word List 23b

1) Ask students to form words that begin with the S sound.
Examples:

Sack	Saturday	Sue	Scissors	Sad	Serve
Suit	Sea gull	Safe	Set	Sum	Seashell
Said	Sew	Sun	Seat belt	Sale	Sick
Surf	Sea World	Salt	Side	Saddle	Second
Sam	Sign	Sailboat	Secret	Same	Sing
Sailor	Selfish	Sand	Sink	Salad	Seven
Sang	Sir	Sally	Sidewalk	Sank	Sit
Sandal	Sorry	Sat	Site	Sandwich	Sunday
Save	Size	Satin	Sunshine	Saw	So
Saving	Siren	Seed	Seal	Soup	Song
Sea	Sent	Sock	Soft	Salt	Star

Tt   T Sound   24a

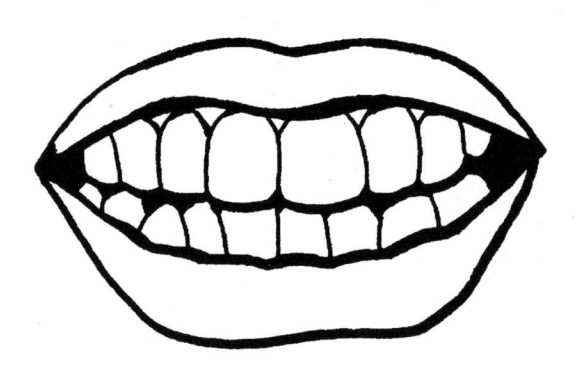

Turkey   **Turtle**   **Teeth**

Tt T Sound Word List 24b

1) Ask students to form words that begin with the T sound.
Examples:

Tack	Ton	Tarzan	Tonight	Tag	Tongue
Tasty	Toothbrush	Tail	Too	Taxi	Toothpaste
Take	Took	Tea bag	Toothpick	Tall	Tool
Teacher	Towel	Tan	Tooth	Teapot	Tower
Tank	Top	Teddy	T-shirt	Tape	Tore
Teenage	Tuesday	Tar	Toss	Tina	Tugboat
Taught	Touch	Tennis	Tulip	Tax	Tough
Texas	Tuna	Tea	Tour	Tiger	Tablecloth
Teach	Tow	Tiny	Tomorrow	Tear	Town
Tiptoe	Tomato	Teeth	Tom	Tug	Tub
Ten	Toe	Taco	Target	Toast	Tire
Tadpole	Tell	Talk	Tent	Table	Toss

Uu   Long Vowel Sound   25a

United States   **Unicorn**

Uu   Long Vowel Sound Word List   25b

1) Ask students to form words that begin with the long vowel sound of U.
Examples:

Unique	Usual	Use	University	Unicorn

2) Ask students to form words that rhyme with the words listed below:

Cue – you, true, glue, due, Sue, blue, chew, do, few, flu, grew, hue, knew, zoo
Cute – flute, suit, jute, mute, chute, fruit, lute, root, scoot, newt, boot, hoot, brute
Mule – rule, fuel, jewel, cruel, tool, cool, drool, fool, spool, stool, pool, school
Use - blues, bruise, clues, cruise, dues, fuse, lose, moos, news, screws, views, ooze
Rude - cued, dude, feud, food, glued, mood, prude, stewed, sued, viewed

Uu   Short Vowel Sound   26a

Umpire   Umbrella

Uu Short Vowel Sound Word List   26b

1) Ask students to form words that begin with the short vowel sound of U.
Examples:

Umpire	Uncle	Unlock	Ugly	Untie	Upstairs
Upset	Us	Unable	Unbelievable	Undecided	Underline
Understand	Unload	Until	Unusual	Under	Unhappy

2) Ask students to form words that rhyme with the words listed below:

Bun – done, fun, none, one, run, son, spun, sun, ton, won, shun, begun, outdone
Gum – chum, crumb, drum, chum, hum, mum, numb, plum, some, thumb
Luck – buck, duck, puck, tuck, cluck, shuck, chuck, pluck, yuk, struck, stuck, truck
Ugh – rug, slug, dug, hug, jug, lug, mug, tug, chug, plug, drug, snug, bug
Cub – sub, grub, rub, tub, shrub, club, hub, scrub, stub, dub

Vv   V Sound   27a

Vegetables   Van   Vacuum

Vv V Sound Word List 27b

**1) Ask students to form words that begin with the V sound.
Examples:**

Vacuum	Variety	Victor	Very	Valley	Vary
Vent	Vest	Value	Vegetable	Verb	Vet
Vanilla	Vein	Verbal	Veterinarian	Variety	Veil
Verse	Veto	Vanish	Vicky	Vertical	Vibrate
Victory	Video	View	Village	Villain	Vine
Vinegar	Violet	Violin	Vision	Vitamin	Vocabulary
Voice	Volume	Vote	Vowel	Velvet	Vehicle

Ww   W Sound

28a

Worm   **Whale**   **Watch**

Ww W Sound Word List 28b

1) Ask students to form words that begin with the W sound.
Examples:

Wag	Wash	Were	With	Wage	Watch
West	Woke	Waist	Wave	Wet	Won't
Wait	Wax	Wide	Woke	Wake	Way
Wife	Woods	Walk	We	Wild	Words
Wall	Weak	Will	Work	Warm	Wealth
Wind	World	Was	Web	Wing	Would
Wash	Weed	Wink	Wow	Waste	Weight
Wipe	Waffle	Watch	Weird	Wire	Wagon
Wave	Well	Wish	Walrus	Why	White

Xx Yy Zz

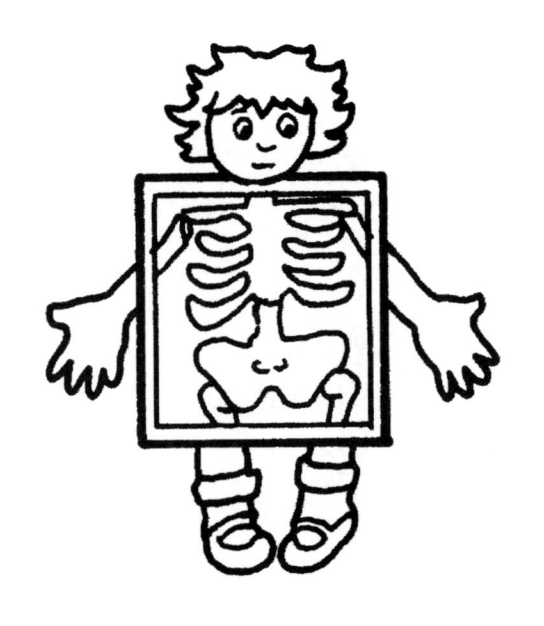

29a

X-Ray **Y**arn **Z**ebra

Xx Yy Zz

1) Ask students to form words that begin with the X sound / Y sound / Z sound.
Examples:

Xx Sound
XL (Extra large)

Yy Sound
Yacht	Young	Yawn	Yard	Yardstick	Your
Yellow	Yell	Yarn	You	Yesterday	Yogurt

Zz Sound
Zebra	Zigzag	Zipper	Zone	Zero	Zucchini
Zip	Zoo	Zookeeper	Zip-Code	Zip-lock	Zillion

Phonemic Awareness Activity Prompt Card

Use the following category prompts to assist your students in identifying words that begin with their target sounds. These prompts may also be used to expand oral expressive vocabulary skills.

5 Senses	**Places to go**	**Descriptions**	**Events**	**Transportation**	**Activities you do**
Hear	Towns	Colors	Birthday Parties	Land	Home
See	States	Sizes		Air	School
Feel	Countries	Shape	**Things in the**	Water	Friends
Taste	Landmarks	Texture	**House**		Park
Smell	Vacation spots		Toys	**Things at School**	Vacation
		Things on TV /	Furniture	Class room	
People	**Food**	**Movies**	Kitchen	Playground	**Things you hear**
Names	Breakfast	Shows	Closet	Hallways	Music
Jobs	Lunch	Cartoons	Bedroom	Supplies	Outside
Family	Dinner	Commercials	Bathroom		
Famous	Snacks		Garage	**Things you wear**	**Animals**
Teachers	Fruit	**Sports**	Yard		Pets
Actors	Drinks	School		**Parts of your**	Farm
Bands		Professional	**Games**	**body**	Jungle
	Books	Olympics	Board		Ocean
	Characters		Card		Zoo
	Settings		Inside		
	Pictures		Outside		

Notes:

Notes: